MAKING SIX FIGURES WITH NFT ART WITHOUT BEING A MAJOR TRADER

Practical Steps of Selling NFT ART, Minting, Collecting, and Changing Your Life for Better

Copyright

© 2022 Nijel James. All rights reserved.

No permission is given for any part of this book to be reproduced, transmitted in any form or means; electronic or mechanical, stored in a retrieval system, photocopied, recorded, scanned, or otherwise. Any of these actions require the proper written permission of the publisher.

Copyright protected with ProtectMyWork.com Reference Number: (To be Updated).

ISBN: (To be Updated) (ebook)

ISBN: 978-1-7396635-1-3 (paperback)

MEET THE AUTHOR

A writer and a successful trader based in the United Kingdom with over ten years of experience. The author of *MAKING SIX FIGURES WITH NFT ART WITHOUT BEING A MAJOR TRADER.*

Nijel James, is passionate about the digital world, cryptocurrency, and blockchain networks. He writes this book to introduce the concept of metaverse, clear its misconceptions, and share simple ways to invest wisely in it by buying into the future.

MEET THE AUTHOR 3

DISCLAIMER 6

INTRODUCTION 7

CHAPTER ONE 10

Understanding NFTs 10

    Fungible and Non-fungible Assets 12

        Characteristics of NFTs 12

CHAPTER TWO 20

Digital Art, Digital Collector, and Digital Creator 20

    Characteristics of an NFT Marketplace 24

CHAPTER THREE 30

Monetizing NFTs 30

    How to Create NFTs 31

        How To Buy NFTs 34

        How to Sell NFT 36

CHAPTER FOUR 43

Top NFT Marketplaces 43

    How to Link NFT and ETH 46

CHAPTER FIVE 51

Problems Confronting NFT 51

Theft and Loss of Cryptocurrencies 57

Selling Your NFT Without Delay 60

CONCLUSION 70

DISCLAIMER

All knowledge contained in this book is given for informational and educational purposes only. The author is not in any way accountable for any results or outcomes that emanate from using this material. Constructive attempts have been made to provide information that is both accurate and effective, but the author is not bound for the accuracy or use/misuse of this information.

INTRODUCTION

NFTs are currently the hottest subject in the digital world. You must have heard about them before arriving here. The growth in the NFT market and its frequent mention by mainstream media have surprised many people in the crypto space.

At the beginning of 2021, an NFT was sold for $69 million, shocking the NFT industry. NFTs may be the killer blockchain product that will lead to further adoption of the crypto industry.

There are many reasons for the popularity of non-fungible tokens that are driving their uses.

Several people believe they are new types of digital assets. In contrast, others think of them as the next step in evolving cryptocurrencies.

Over the past several months, NFT sales have increased significantly. It all started with Dapper Lab's NBA Top Shot virtual trading cards, which featured video highlights of top NBA games. The virtual trading cards were an instant success, garnered colossal recognition, and marked one of the first successful forays of sports organizations into NFTs. Thousands of NBA fans have turned their passion for the league into a new fan economy by collecting digital cards featuring their favorite stars or athletic moments.

Not long after NBA Top Shot took off, craftsmen additionally went to NFTs as another passage to advertising and adapting their specialty. One of the chief closeout houses, Christie's, further legitimized the workmanship of NFT development by teaming up with NFT specialists to unload their fine art.

During the crypto bull market of 2020–2021, crypto natives were looking for a way to signal their status and wealth online, particularly on Reddit, Discord, and Twitter. Digital avatars, like CryptoPunks, have rapidly soared in value as digital personas have grown in importance.

NFTs have given creators worldwide another option to get paid for their work.

The impact of NFTs hasn't been limited to the artistic community. In the gaming industry, NFTs allow for creating a new "Play to Earn" model, which is in contrast to the traditional concept of players paying for games.

In terms of originality and adaptability, NFTs have a lot more to offer than just skyrocketing prices. To understand the recent upswing, we'll go into the depths of the NFT realm.

This eBook is a sincere attempt by the author to help learners come to terms with non-fungible tokens or NFTs. The target audience is NFT beginners with little or no idea about NFTs, with step-by-step guides on buying, selling, storing, and minting NFTs.

Let's explore further about NFTs by deciphering the fundamental ideas that underpin them, the history of NFTs, and the fundamentals of NFTs.

The fundamentals of NFTs would include an overview of their definition alongside the essential elements in their design. You will also find a clear overview of the NFT marketplace and wallets, which are popular in present times. This eBook also explores the practical ramifications of non-fungible tokens, such as how to create, purchase, and trade them. Let us jump right into the first chapter on NFTs.

CHAPTER ONE

Understanding NFTs

What Are NFTs?

To understand the importance and usefulness of NFTs, you would necessarily need an explanation of NFTs.

Non-fungible tokens are primarily digital assets with feature identifying information documented in smart contracts. There is a clear motivation for learning about NFTs from varying usage scenarios evolving in the present times.

Non-fungible tokens, often known as NFTs, are one of the trendiest phenomena in the blockchain and crypto code worlds. If you look more deeply into the concepts of NFTs, you'll find that they're essentially one-of-a-kind digital codes. The one-of-a-kind digital codes are built on the same blockchain technology as cryptocurrencies like Ethereum.

NFTs, on the other hand, are unique in that they grant you ownership of digital goods. The presence of NFTs on a blockchain is compelling evidence of the NFT blockchain interaction. As an added benefit, you can purchase and sell NFTs with cryptocurrencies.

Surprisingly, NFTs do not require a physical asset in the actual world to function. They include the representation of physical entities such as artwork, real estate, and even your pet rabbit.

An NFT is a token that possesses a unique identifier and has additional parameters that allow you to store certain information. A token's non-fungibility is due to this unique identification. The extra data can be any data such as content, pictures, sound, and video files. One of the preeminent perspectives you should note when learning about NFTs is the basic concept of non-fungibility fundamental to their design. You have to know the distinction between fungibility and non-fungibility to understand how NFTs are interesting as resources. The fundamental concepts encompassing NFTs summarize the contrast between fungible and non-fungible assets as a matter of reality.

Fungible and Non-fungible Assets

In straightforward terms, a fungible good is an item that's commonly conversely related with another. Money could be a great case. A $500 bill is worth the same as other $500 bills (or ten $50 bills). Despite minor differences such as serial numbers and issue dates, notes are considered fungible as they are interchangeable and encourage exchanges in our daily activities.

On the other hand, vehicles, craftsmanship, and properties are illustrations of non-fungible things that are unique and not equivalent to one another.

Think of two buildings found beside each other. They may dwell inside the same neighborhood, share the same property designer, and are indeed seen as indistinguishable from the exterior. Still, they are, in fact, not comparable nor interchangeable. Their stylistic layout and insides format may be diverse. One can be closer to a high-traffic train station, making it more important than the other. Unlike two $500 bills, these two houses do not share the same inherent value. They are not commonly interchangeable, making them non-fungible.

Characteristics of NFTs

In essential words, NFTs are computerized tokens on a blockchain network and give a representation of a unique item. You'll be able to discover a precise clarification of NFTs by looking at their imperative qualities within the following discussions:

Uniqueness

The first quality of non-fungible tokens is uniqueness. The data within the code of NFTs outlines the properties of the tokens in detail, subsequently separating them from others.

NFTs are one-of-a-kind and not interchangeable, unlike fungible cryptocurrencies. You can freely exchange Bitcoin on cryptocurrency exchanges because it is identical and indistinguishable.

Regardless, because no two NFTs are the same, you cannot easily exchange one. NFTs have distinct characteristics, distinguishing each piece even though they appear similar on the surface. For instance, a computerized art may have data about individual pixels within the code of its NFT.

Traceability

The on-chain documentation of exchanges for an NFT incorporates all subtle elements of the NFT. You'll effortlessly follow the history of NFTs from the time of their creation till the display time. It is additionally conceivable to recognize the different times when the non-fungible token changed hands. Hence, you'll effectively confirm the realness of NFTs with the traceability characteristic.

Indivisibility

Another imperative highlight you'll note within the NFT marketplace is its unbreakable quality.

Unlike traditional cryptocurrencies, NFTs cannot be broken into smaller units. You may not buy half of the work of art, which applies to NFTs. You cannot execute with NFTs as divisions of a total NFT because it is outlandish to partition NFTs into littler categories.

Some projects however, allow NFTs to be fractionalized into smaller, more fungible parts. Allowing clients to own portions of an NFT rather than the entire piece, therefore lowering the section boundary for high-priced NFTs, and advancing the liquidity of these securities.

Scarcity

Non-fungible tokens include shortages that can move forward their engaging quality to buyers. As a result, the resources would be exceedingly alluring and guarantee that the supply does not outperform the request.

Programmability

The foremost vital characteristic of NFTs that will drive numerous other NFT applications in the future is programmability. NFTs' feature-complete programmability is comparable to conventional advanced resources and tokens on savvy contract blockchains. Clients can include highlights to their NFTs agreeing to their inclinations. After all, NFTs are essentially pieces of code, and you'll be able to add anything to the code. These preferences of NFT make this innovation indeed more profitable.

History of NFTs

NFTs began making news in 2021. There are numerous reasons to consider 2021 as "NFTs' Year" with a mind-boggling development rate. Makers found the opportunity to monetize their work, whereas collectors found an effective strategy for obtaining and putting away value.

When Did It All Begin?

Many of you would be quick to bring within the title of the Ethereum blockchain. You're not off-base, as the lion's share of NFTs is built on the Ethereum blockchain. You ought to note that the concept of NFTs has existed for a long time before the advent of Ethereum.

2012–2013: The First NFTs (Colored Coins)

The colored Coins concept depicted a course of strategies to encourage the representation and administration of real-world resources on the Bitcoin blockchain. It was first presented in a paper by Meni Rosenfeld issued on the Bitcoin blockchain on December 4, 2012.

In expansion, Colored Coins offer assistance in demonstrating possession of the real-world resources spoken to on the Bitcoin blockchain. The Colored Coins are standard Bitcoins, although they have a unique stamp for recognizable proof. In any case, the concept never saw the light of day due to certain restrictions with Bitcoin.

2014-2016: Ethereum Makes Its NFT Debut

The following noteworthy stage in NFT history arrived between 2014 and 2016. Bitcoin blockchain ruled a significant share of advancement and experimentation concerning NFTs. In any case, Ethereum gave an adaptable elective for NFT improvement during this time before developing as the favorite for NFTs.

Ethereum, a digital isometric environment where people can own tiles, mine them for blocks, and build stuff, was one of the first NFTs on the Ethereum network. The project was launched in 2015 and has become a sought-after collectible due to its role in Ethereum's history. At that point, the age of memes arrived in 2016, and Uncommon Pepes NFTs began making a few commotions on the counterparty.

The move toward Ethereum began since Bitcoin clients did not acknowledge the thought of filling up square space with tokens speaking to the possession of tokens. The entry of Ethereum in 2014 spelled positive news for the NFT scene. Ethereum blockchain presented a particular collection of token measures which empowered the improvement of tokens. NFT engineers seem to effectively use the token measures to manage the strategies for development, issuing, and deploying new tokens.

2017 – Getting Noticed

The most well-known brand in today's NFT is the market that came with the advent of Cryptopunks in 2017. The project used the ERC 20 (Ethereum Request Comment) standard to generate 10,000 unique characters. Given the historical value and rarity of Cryptopunk NFTs and the growing popularity of NFTs in 2021, there is enough reason for them to be overvalued. Cryptopunk NFT sold for $530 million, one of NFT's most prominent sales ever.

The next big step in NFT history was CryptoKitties in 2017. Cryptokitties is a blockchain-based virtual game where you can pet virtual cats and trade them. Based on the Ethereum blockchain, CryptoKitties rose to fame after its debut at the world's largest hackathon for Ethereum. The CryptoKitties craze has reached the point where people have started making unreal profits by trading virtual cats. At one point, activity on CryptoKitties clogged the Ethereum network, forcing the blockchain giant to think about scaling. CryptoKitties showed the world how capable NFT is.

2018-2020: NFT, Now A Well Known Brand

This recent period of NFT history heralds the rise of NFT-based games. Between 2018 and 2020, NFT began to gain public attention, mainly through NFT-related games and metaverse initiatives.

Decentraland, an Ethereum-based virtual reality platform, was one of the most popular among the NFT games. It features environments for players to explore, develop and play, collect items, and more. Many others have followed suit and created new NFTs' applications in the gaming industry. For example, Enjin Coin allows tokenization of game items on Ethereum. You can't miss Axie Infinity's name, which made a big splash during the COVID19 lockdown, especially in the Philippines.

2021-Today: Outstanding Development

Today the world has seen many new types of NFTs with different applications. In the long run, the growth of the metaverse could make the NFT an essential component of every individual's digital presence.

This detailed account of the history of the NFT shows that the NFT has flourished in a reasonably short time. As a result, one inevitably wonders what the world of NFTs looks like right now. You can find the correct answers to such questions by thinking about the NFT ecosystem.

CHAPTER TWO

Digital Art, Digital Collector, and Digital Creator

Digital art refers to a digitized art or virtual art.

Digital art is scanned, drawn, or computer-generated and utilizes technology to create and present artistic works. Digital art is vital in filming and advertisement. As you are aware that we live in a digital world now, digital art is more needed than ever. NFTs serve as a stepping stone for creating and collecting digital art.

Artists can use NFT to create programmable art, hence become a digital creator.

Digital creators can program their work to change or behave differently depending on certain factors. The purpose of NFTs is to show off your work. Digital artists now have access to a whole new world thanks to NFTs. Due to the simplicity with which a user can copy an image online, selling digital art is challenging. The NFT procedure, on the other hand, allows creators to get credit for their work and sell it.

Before making a purchase, buyers can check the authenticity of digital art. Creative theft is a significant issue, and digital creators can help combat it.

Viewing NFTs is analogous to seeing an original work of art at a museum. You may appreciate it so much that you purchase a print from the museum store for your house, but the original will remain on display.

The format's unique ownership allows buyers and collectors of NFTs to benefit from it. The thrill of possessing an original work of art attracts collectors. They might also be able to gain from the sale of public-use rights.

Another good news for digital creators is that NFTs have a feature that you can enable to ensure that every time your NFT is sold or changes hands, you'll get some of that benefit if your work gets super popular and increases in value.

In short, NFTs provide digital creators and collectors with three distinct benefits:

I. Value

ii. **Exclusive ownership**

iii. **Security**

Terminologies and Principles of the NFT Marketplace

Like you go to the markets and malls to buy other commodities, you need a place to buy and sell NFTs. NFT marketplaces offer a secured environment for displaying and brokering the files. NFT marketplaces provide a gateway for users to sell and purchase digital assets, including art and music.

There are some principles that NFT marketplaces follow to ensure a secure and friendly environment for digital creators and collectors. You will need to understand the terminologies and regulations used in NFTs marketplaces for smooth usage of the platforms.

Crypto Wallets

To get involved with NFTs on various marketplaces, buyers and sellers need crypto wallets - a place to hold your cryptocurrencies. You will be able to buy NFTs and trade cryptocurrencies when you add a wallet to a store or exchange. Note that you'll find a lot of wallets out there, so do some research before choosing the one that's right for you. NFTs or digital currency are stored differently on a hard drive in these apps. They contain data and metadata pointing to where the owner's files are stored on the blockchain. For a broader client base, marketplaces work with several crypto wallet providers like MyEtherWallet or WalletConnect.

Auctions and Sales

In the actual world, marketplaces serve the same purpose as art galleries. You can sell objects at a set price. Auctions for new art or works by well-known artists might be scheduled on marketplaces.

Smart Contracts

In NFT markets, smart contracts specify the terms of a transaction between a buyer and a seller. These terms are enshrined in a self-executing digitized contract based on the blockchain. The contract becomes binding and irreversible when the buyer accepts the seller's terms.

Costs of Operation

Users frequently overlook the fees associated with digital transactions. Blockchain transactions, on the other hand, consume a lot of energy. The cost of NFTs may also include the energy expenses of facilitating the transaction over the network and exchanging money into crypto.

Characteristics of an NFT Marketplace

Trading on NFT marketplaces should not be a tedious process. NFT markets are built for a fantastic user experience, making it easy to find what you're looking for and handle sophisticated transactions. NFTs marketplaces frequently have the following characteristics:

The shopfront

The digital arts and descriptions are displayed in a storefront, verifying the files' authenticity and legitimacy. The storefront includes a chart detailing the rarity of NFTs.

The Search Tool

OpenSea, one of the first NFT marketplaces, is a broad market that accepts any NFT. The focus of newer marketplaces is typically on a specific niche. Using the search function, buyers may quickly and conveniently look for and purchase anything posted on marketplaces.

The use of Filters

Another method marketplaces improve a buyer's experience is through search filters. Collectors and investors have various standards when it comes to NFTs. Users can arrange products by categories such as price, rarity, and artist using the filter tool.

The Listing

The NFT marketplace gives buyers and sellers a pleasurable experience through its listing process. When someone wishes to list a file, the marketplaces offer a simple step-by-step process that includes explicit uploading instructions.

The Listing's Status

The method is disclosed to both parties in an NFT transaction. The marketplace displays information for vendors, such as the number of visitors and bids a file has gotten. Once someone makes an offer, the websites notify you. Before completing a purchase, buyers are informed of the verification details.

The Purchase and Auctioning

Users can sell in NFT marketplaces in a variety of ways. Timed auctions are often the most significant way famous artists get the best pricing. The competition can quickly drive up the price. On the other hand, direct purchasing and selling is a more convenient and straightforward option.

The Wallet

The NFT marketplace provides crypto wallet solutions to customers, allowing easy buying and selling and a secure way to store your cryptos and NFTs.

Evaluations

For both buyers and sellers, ratings are a helpful tool. NFT marketplaces allow you to score your buying experience with a seller since consumers are more willing to conduct business with someone who has a good reputation. The grading system also prevents negative behaviors like making misleading representations or cancelling a transaction before the smart contract.

Understanding NFTs as Collectibles and Digital Assets

Humanity progressed as a species, and what we acquired moved with it. It is stated that the desire to collect originates from a need for esteem at a young age. Developing a passion for possession and control explains why children gather fragile toys from an early age.

This drive follows us throughout our lives, and as a result, the things we collect vary. Collecting takes on new meaning as a source of pleasure and, in some instances, a status symbol. It can be a way to show our support for a specific point, object, or fandom.

Automobiles, observatories, and stamps are examples of cards, money, and comic books.

Digital collectibles, viewed as NFTs, are online. Today, acrylic box frames of figurines stacked to the rafters and endless shelves of unfilled shelves are slowly dying out. Instead of dedicating a room to your passion, you can now carry your massive collection around in your hand. Digital collectibles do not only save space but can also improve relationships. You won't have to be arguing with your partner about putting up one more shelf for your figurines.

Collecting is in our blood, but the world of traditional fungible goods is being turned upside down by a previously undiscovered universe of digital collectibles. NFTs are a long-standing notion that is now gaining attention in the mainstream media.

Digital assets can be models, works of art, music, tweets, or anything else that can be purchased as a collectible because they are non-fungible tokens. It's essentially a new method to display your affection for your favorite films, TV series, bands, sports, etc. Load your boots with digital toys, posters, games, and more instead of actual stuff you're unlikely to use or even take out of the bag.

Collecting NFTs is fun to do. The allure of social interaction is constantly present. Alternatively, if you're investing, the earlier you buy something, the longer it has to appreciate. As the trend rises, so does your profit.

Furthermore, NFTs are limitless; any fandom from any world area can be turned into one. The list goes on and on with movies, comic books, art, music, designer apparel, et cetera.

There's no question that digital collectibles are the future. Thousands of them are already available for purchase, collection, and enjoyment across the globe. There is already a large community surrounding digital collectibles, so they will be around for the foreseeable future. It is still possible to buy, trade, and sell digital collectibles just like real-life ones. The trend of turning collectibles for a profit daily is encouraging. Your fandom will be more likely to be able to create their own digital collectibles if more people are interested in digital collectibles. NFTs offer an additional method to promote something you care about, and many people are currently doing so.

CHAPTER THREE

Monetizing NFTs

The basic knowledge regarding non-fungible tokens offered thus far gives a vivid picture of the NFTs realm. However, one can question the optimal techniques for interacting with NFTs in the real world and making money.

How would you go about making an NFT? Many people would immediately suggest NFT minting as a viable solution.

Yes, NFTs can be minted! But how?

The next question, of course, is how to sell the NFTs you make. NFT marketplaces are the obvious solution.

"How can you sell NFTs on the marketplaces of your choice?" is the point here, emphasizing techniques for obtaining NFTs.

How to Create NFTs

1. The first point to remember is that building an NFT is a simple and straightforward process. The creator should select the blockchain on which their NFTs will be issued.
2. Ethereum is currently one of the most obvious options for minting NFTs, owing to its widespread use. In addition, several other blockchain networks provide viable opportunities to create NFTs.
3. Binance Smart Chain, Cosmos, Tron, Polkadot, and Tezos, for example, are several blockchain networks that have lately gained traction in the NFT sector.

Token standards, marketplaces, and wallet services are entirely separate from the blockchain networks used to create NFTs. You'll need the following items to make NFTs or use the NFT minting technique:

1. An ERC-721 supported Ethereum wallets, such as Enjin, Coinbase Wallet, or Metamask.
2. $50-$100 worth of ETH tokens which can be bought on exchanges like Coinbase in exchange for fiat currency.
3. After that, you'll need a marketplace to complete the NFT.

Didn't we just talk about the marketplace and wallets? Yes, but we didn't talk about how to use them. Let's get started on your first NFT piece.

Many marketplaces exist to assist you in connecting your wallets and uploading the photographs you wish to convert to NFTs.

On OpenSea, here's an example of the steps you'll need to take to make NFT art.

- Click on the "create" button in the upper-right corner of the OpenSea application. (Note that the process of uploading an NFT on OpenSea is slightly different from other NFT platforms. You have to create a collection first.)
- You would have to connect to an Ethereum-based wallet with the prompt on the next screen. Enter the wallet password and connect to the NFT marketplace.
- Just click the "create" button and find "my collections."
- After clicking on the "my collections", you must tap the blue "create" button.
- Then, you can upload the image and add your name alongside writing a description. Assign the logo for

your collection, which will be visible on the left side of the screen.

➤ You can add further information to your collection, such as links to social media profiles, a category to make your item discoverable on OpenSea, and a banner image by choosing the pencil icon available on the top right.

➤ You are ready to create an NFT by clicking on "Add New Item" alongside signing a message with the wallet.

➤ Upload your file to convert it to an NFT. It could be an image in jpg or png or a video in mp4 or gif format. You can name and describe it as well. There is an option to add an external link to your NFT, probably that of your personal website.

➤ Next, give your NFT a level based on your desired traits, and it will show up as a progress bar. The attributes could be speed, strength, etc. Adding levels for your NFT is entirely optional.

➤ It is also possible to add numerical stats to your NFT. This is similar to levels, but it won't show up as a progress bar but instead will appear simply as numbers. If the NFT contains explicit or sensitive content, you may categorize it.

- Finally, it's time to mint the NFT. Hit "create.", and you can complete the NFT minting process.
- The next page will show your newly uploaded NFT. From here, you may visit or edit it.

How To Buy NFTs

Buying NFTs is more straightforward than creating or selling NFTs. To buy NFTs, you have to select the marketplace where you want to buy NFTs. We'll be using Opensea as an example. Follow the following steps to purchase your NFTs on OpenSea:

- Create an account on OpenSea if you don't have one already, skip this step if you have an account with OpenSea.
- Connect your blockchain wallet to your NFT account by tapping on the wallet icon in the top right corner. Some of the methods available include MetaMask, Bitski, Fortmatic, and Coinbase Wallet. In this example, we will be using MetaMask.
- When you click the MetaMask button, you'll be asked to connect your wallet to OpenSea. Simply select which MetaMask wallet you would like to connect,

hit "Next", and tap "Connect". You've now established a MetaMask connection to OpenSea.
- ➢ Fund your blockchain wallet with Ethereum or another supported cryptocurrency. You can buy from a crypto exchange.
- ➢ Browse through the marketplace listings and choose the NFT you want to buy.
- ➢ After finding an NFT that suits your liking, it's time to purchase it. Hit the "Buy now" button.
- ➢ A MetaMask validation will prompt you to validate or refute the operation.
- ➢ If you click on the "Edit" button, there will be the option to increase or decrease the Max fee. Increasing it will hasten the transaction while reducing it will cause the transaction to take longer to confirm. When you're done, click on Save and then Confirm.
- ➢ There you have it. You have purchased an NFT from OpenSea. Now, it's time to view your new purchase. Simply head to your profile, and the NFT will be available for viewing.

Alternatively, you can participate in the action/bidding process of your chosen NFTs. However, you may or may not own the NFT based on the bidding amount, as the highest bidder gets the NFT.

How to Sell NFT

Just like buying NFT, you need a marketplace to sell your NFT. There are two ways to sell NFT.

1. First, you can buy NFT on one platform and sell it on another.
2. Second, you can create an NFT and auction it for sale on the same marketplace.

➢ To sell an NFT, you need to create one first, as discussed earlier. The basic procedures of selling your NFT are outlined here.

➢ Create an account on OpenSea or any other marketplace and connect your funded or to be funded blockchain wallet.

➢ Mint the object you want to sell into an NFT by uploading it to your account.

➢ Pay the minimum fees for creating NFTs on the marketplace. This varies from marketplace to marketplace. OpenSea doesn't charge to create NFTs. You'll only pay a one-time gas fee for making your first NFT; the rest are free. If the marketplace uses Ethereum NFTs, you will need "gas" to create the tokens. Gas costs are the fees given to miners in

return for the computer power they use to record transactions on the blockchain.
- ➢ Once uploaded, select the NFT you want to sell and set a fixed price or a bidding range.
- ➢ To attract potential consumers, advertise your NFT on social media.

You get paid automatically once a buyer purchases your NFT, generally through bidding.

You can also add the option of royalties to your NFTs, which can help you fetch a share of earnings from future sales of your NFTs.

How to Invest In NFTs

With all the information and news about NFTs, you will be wondering if you should invest in NFTs. We'll now be looking at how you can invest in NFTs.

Step 1: Research Valuable NFTs

Your primary focus should be on selecting an NFT that you believe has future value potential. What does the NFT have to offer? Does it give the buyer access to exclusive bonus content or boost the online status of the buyer?

Consider the following factors when determining the value of an **NFT:**

- **Usage or utility:** how the NFT is used, such as a token used in gaming.
- **Ownership history:** how famous the creator is.
- **Future value:** entails predicting where the NFT will go in the future.
- **Liquidity premium:** the amount of demand for the art among NFTs, with increased traffic leading to increased premiums.

Keep the date of the sale, the coin requirements, and the number of NFTs offered in mind while looking at future NFTs. This will help you understand the rarity of the choice you've made.

The following are some details of the NFT that you should double-check:

- **Who are the creators:** you want a respected team to assist in increasing the NFT's worth.
- **If it's on-chain or off-chain:** off-chain relies on centralized servers. The image will be lost if the server crashes.

Keep an eye out for NFTs that are held entirely off-chain. You must be confident that the supervisor can be trusted with your vital NFT. You'll also want to join the

NFT's Telegram chats to learn more about the brand and understand what others are saying about this particular line of NFTs.

Step 2: Purchase Cryptocurrency

To obtain the NFT, you must first acquire digital money. Most NFTs are purchased with Ethereum, but there are a few exceptions. You may buy Ethereum and other digital currencies at crypto brokers or exchanges such as Coinbase (COIN), Binance, Gemini, Etoro, or Kraken, among other crypto exchanges.

Cryptocurrency Broker

A company or individual who acts as an intermediary to facilitate the purchase and sale of cryptocurrency. Buyers and sellers also trade with each other online, depending on current market circumstances.

When purchasing cryptocurrencies, consider that fees are an essential factor to consider. For a trade of $10 or less, Coinbase, for example, charges $0.99. The larger the transaction, the higher the cost. For crypto trading, SoFi Active Invest costs up to 1.25 percent.

Fees can be a flat rate per transaction or a percentage of an account's 30-day transaction volume. Examine costs based on the transaction sizes you intend to undertake to determine how much you'll spend.

Step 3: Purchase Your NFT From A Marketplace

Purchasing an NFT from a marketplace should be a piece of cake for you now. You can decide to sell the item for a flat rate or hold an auction for the token.

Be sure that you have enough crypto to complete the transaction without incurring any substantial costs. Expenses might include the costs of obtaining and exchanging cryptos, as well as the costs of converting one crypto to another and gas.

Remember that the recorded price or the most recent offer for an NFT isn't the total purchase price. For example, because of gas costs, the final cost of an NFT valued at $40 in Ethereum could reach $150 to $200.

How Do You Make Profit?

The essence of an investment is to make a profit, right? Now is the time to reap from the research you made before investing in your NFT. You can make a profit from your investment in two ways:

By selling your NFTs across platforms, you buy NFT from platform A and sell it on platform B.

Selling your NFT on another marketplace often has a higher resale value. Take, for instance, you purchase your NFT for $180, including gas fees on OpenSea. You can now go to the nifty gateway (another NFT marketplace which you must be aware of its rate) to sell your NFT at a higher price of about $300. Thus, you make a profit of $120. Cool, isn't it? When transacting across marketplaces, you should choose marketplaces with similar modes of payment. For example, OpenSea and Nifty Gateways use Ethereum tokens as means of payment. In contrast, Rarible uses Rari, its own native token. Using marketplaces with different tokens will obviously give you issues.

You can also profit from investing in NFT by holding your NFT.

Suppose you discovered from your research that the NFT has a high upside value potential. You may not sell it immediately and wait till it appreciates at a price to give you much profit. A perfect example of this is CryptoPunk 1422, purchased for $74 back in 2017. However, the NFT was later said to be sold in October 2021 for an incredible $2 million.

That's massive, right? It is easy to make money with valuable NFTs.

CHAPTER FOUR

Top NFT Marketplaces

You will agree that marketplaces are inevitable to make money from NFTs. Hence, it is necessary to discuss the top NFT marketplaces. Let's take a peep at some of them.

OpenSea

OpenSea is the largest NFT marketplace by trading volume. It saw about $3 billion in trading volume in September 2021 alone, making up more than 99% of the total market. It has a wide variety of digital assets on the platform, offering an accessible signup facility.

Founded in December 2017 by Alex Atallah and Devin Finzer, OpenSea is a generalized marketplace set up to facilitate the trading of NFTs. One may mistake OpenSea as a place solely for trading NFT art pieces, but that's far from the truth.

The platform comprises many NFT categories, including digital art, music, domain names, virtual land,

43

trading cards, etc. As of now, OpenSea supports over 150 unique payment tokens and serves as an excellent place for NFT beginners.

> ***The idea to start OpenSea came to Alex and Devin during*** CryptoKitties' surge of popularity. Both founders saw a need for an NFT marketplace to facilitate NFT trades.

SuperRare

SuperRare is a marketplace with highly curated NFTs and is a more community-focused platform. Being highly curated, you can expect the marketplace to work closely with artists and feature a smaller variety of art. SuperRare also has its fungible token named RARE.

Nifty Gateway

Another favorable choice of an NFT marketplace would include Nifty Gateway, owned by Gemini's crypto exchange. Here, users can buy and sell music, sports cards, game items, etc. This marketplace collaborates with various top artists and offers limited edition NFTs. It is famously known for hosting Beeple's $6.6 million sales of CROSSROAD.

Nifty supports MetaMask wallet, and the user will need to pay via their debit or credit card or Ethereum. The platform also offers commissions to the creators.

Rarible

> Rarible is an NFT marketplace that offers various NFTs (e.g., art, video, etc.) and is not content-restricted unlike some platforms. Rarible also has its own native NFT token, RARI, similar to SuperRare, and is part of a larger initiative to decentralize the platform.

The marketplace has promising similarities with OpenSea. The collaboration of Rarible with notable names such as Adobe and Taco Bell speaks a lot for its credibility as an NFT marketplace.

MakersPlace

Another lesser-known NFT exchange would be MakersPlace. They set themselves out from the competitors by promoting "very unique" NFTs. The majority of these are one-of-a-kind manifestations from elite collections. NFT drops have also been held by artists like Shakira and T-Pain on MakersPlace.

Solanart

Catering to your NFT trading needs on the Solana ecosystem is Solanart. Despite being in beta, the marketplace is already actively facilitating trades, including prominent collections such as Degen Ape Academy and Aurory.

Binance NFT

The popular crypto exchange, Binance, has also gotten into the NFT game by setting up its own marketplace. Aptly named Binance NFT, the marketplace allows users to buy and sell Binance Smart Chain and Ethereum NFTs.

Artion

Artion is a new Fantom-based NFT marketplace launched by Andre Cronje. Its source code is open-source, and unlike other marketplaces, Artion does not charge any platform fees for mints and purchases.

How to Link NFT and ETH

The most common token used in creating, selling and buying NFTs is Ethereum (ETH). Ethereum provides the following benefits to NFTs:

It is easy to confirm ownership provenance because transaction history and token information are publicly verifiable.

It is practically impossible to "steal" ownership of a transaction once it's been confirmed.

Trading NFTs can be done peer-to-peer without requiring platforms willing to take massive commissions as compensation.

Ethereum goods all have the same meta-data. Additionally, all Ethereum products are interconnected, resulting in NFTs transferable. An NFT can be purchased on one product and sold on another. You can list your NFTs on several items as a creator, and each product will have the most up-to-date ownership information.

Ethereum will never crash, implying that your investment will never lose value., meaning your tokens will always be available to sell.

All of these explains the need for ETH wallets in the world of NFTs.

There are many Ethereum based token wallets used in minting and transacting NFTs, and they include:

MetaMask

The all-around wallet for anything related to Ethereum is Metamask. It allows storage of ETH tokens, ERC-721, and ERC-20 tokens. The foremost advantage of Metamask points to the ease of interfacing with popular NFT marketplaces such as Rarible and OpenSea.

Trust Wallet

Trust wallet is one of the most secured crypto wallets that offers to buy, store, exchange, and earn cryptocurrencies. At this moment, this wallet supports more than 40 blockchain platforms and 160k+ digital assets. It also supports storing ERC-721 and ERC-1155 tokens. Users can use the Trust wallet in OpenSea and Rarible marketplaces.

Enjin Wallet

Another outstanding choice of NFT wallet would refer to Enjin Wallet. The wallet supports additional support for ERC-1155 token standards. Therefore, Enjin Wallet can provide the advantage of additional value in compatibility.

In addition, the multiple functionalities such as trading, commercial centers, and the dApp program make it a competitive choice of wallets for NFTs.

SNow you have different components for participating in the world of NFTs. You know the significance and role of wallets. The question now is, how do you link your NFT and ETH, right?

Linking your NFT and ETH is pretty easy; just follow the steps below:

Setup Coinbase or any other online platform for buying cryptocurrencies.

Next, buy ETH in Coinbase and create a wallet for your ETH.

Now you can use Coinbase to transfer funds (ETH) into your **MetaMask wallet.**

To link your wallet, tap on my wallet. You will find the icon in the top right corner. Some of the methods available include MetaMask, Bitski, Fortmatic, and Coinbase Wallet. Let's use MetaMask as an example.

Select the MetaMask symbol, and you will be asked to link your wallet to OpenSea. Simply select which MetaMask wallet you would like to link.

Hit "Next", and tap "Connect" and follow the on screen commands. Some platforms have a QR code which makes it even easier to link. You have now directly linked your ETH to Opensea via MetaMask.

CHAPTER FIVE

Problems Confronting NFT

Now that you are familiar with minting and trading NFTs, you are ready to dip your toes into the waters and start acquiring your very first NFT. Nevertheless, you must be aware of the dangers involved.

The radical growth of NFTs is the foremost factor that causes concerns about the future. Experts have pointed out that NFTs are like Pandora's Box, bringing everything unknown to the world before it.

Obviously, the million-dollar NFT sales might be one of the first things grabbing people's attention NFTs. However, reality has its own way of hitting hard when you expect it the least. NFT has its own problems and challenges posing a threat to NFTs future. We'll be discussing such difficulties and challenges in this chapter.

NFT Scams

One major problem confronting NFTs is the growing NFT scams. Below are a few common NFT scams you should keep an eye out for.

Fake Websites

One of the most rampant NFT scams is replicating NFT project websites or popular marketplaces like OpenSea. Often, unwary users will be prompted to connect their crypto wallets to the fake website to mint or transact with an NFT. In most cases, the action will drain the funds from the users' wallets, whereas the more "fortunate" ones will pay for a fake NFT.

Is there any protection against falling for this scheme? Always double-check all the website links before you click on them. The official links are usually shared in each projects' locked Discord channels (e.g., Announcement or FAQ channels) or on their Twitter page.

Another promising "mint habit" to cultivate is to glance through the comments on the project's social channels as you prepare for a mint. Often, internet sleuths will call out scams, and if you see any, it's best to take a step back and investigate deeper. In cases where you are unsure but still insist on buying or minting an NFT in the hopes of striking gold, connect using a new wallet with just the right amount of funds needed.

Remember, stay safe and always do your own research!

Fake Collections

Don't take anything at face value - if it doesn't seem right, it probably isn't.

The same saying also applies to NFTs, so don't buy that 1 ETH CryptoPunk yet! Be sure to check the NFT is indeed part of the authentic collection and not an imitation product.

Marketplaces such as OpenSea will mark most high-profile collections with a "Verified Collection" tag. Some creative scammers attempt to replicate this by including the verified tick in the fake collection's logo. One quick way to check is to hover over the blue tick on OpenSea, and the words "Verified Collection" should pop up.

If the "Verified Collection" tag isn't present, check the NFT collection's official websites and community channels to determine if the contract addresses match what you're purchasing.

Impersonation

Impersonation scams have been around for a long time and, unfortunately, still prevalent in crypto. Scammers often impersonate the projects' customer support team to prey on unsuspecting users in need of help. Usually, these are phishing attempts to get ahold of the targets' personal details and sensitive information such as their wallet seed phrases.

Fake giveaways are also common scams that entice users to connect their wallets with a phoney website or surrender their private keys. If done successfully, the users' funds will be at the mercy of the scammers, allowing them to drain all of the wallet's assets.

Sophisticated hackers may even bypass security and take control of the project's social media or Discord accounts. This allows hackers to share fake "official links" in "official channels" that can dupe even the most careful users. As in the case of Beeple's Discord group, Artist Derek Laufman discovered someone had created a verified profile in his name to sell his art as NFTs. The impostor account was shut down, but only after purchases had been made, which led to a user losing ~38 ETH. While there is no secure method for staying away from such incidents, you can get your work done by looking at different sources (e.g., Twitter, Discord,

Telegram, and the authority site) before purchasing or stamping any NFTs.

You will receive hundreds of unprompted direct messages (DMs) or spam from other Discord users as you join more and more projects' Discord groups. Don't click on links shared by other users. This is a way scammers share fake websites to steal private information. This was one of the methods that scammers used to trick users in Aurory's high-profile NFT drop.

One way to prevent this is to tweak Discord's privacy settings to prevent direct messages from server members. In this way, all private messages sent by users, not on your friend list will be filtered out.

So while considering your NFT purchase, watch out for scams like doppelganger stores and crypto wallets, counterfeit collectibles and digital art, free giveaways and NFT airdrops.

Lowball Bids

While strictly not a scam, this is still a widespread phenomenon that both aspiring and veteran NFT collectors should note. It is common to receive multiple offers for your NFT, especially for popular collections or rare pieces. When you receive a request for your NFT, pay close attention to the denomination of the cryptocurrency for the offer. Is the offer denominated in ETH, DAI, USDC, or other tokens?

Take the below offer for Poet #3179, for instance. While 1.25 ETH might be a decent offer to consider for the NFT, 1.25 USDC is undoubtedly not. In this case, the bidder hopes that the NFT owner mistakenly accepts the offer for a quick and easy profit, so watch out for these tactics.

Unfortunately, there will always be some bad actors looking to profit from our lapse of judgment, as there are many lucrative businesses out there. NFTs should generally follow the same old cybersecurity practices:

i. Do not disclose your wallet seed message to anyone.

ii. Verify and check the links you click on

iii. Cross-check and verify information across multiple sources

iv. Use a fresh wallet when connecting to dubious sites

v. Always do your own research

Theft and Loss of Cryptocurrencies

Chainalysis estimates that 20% of all Bitcoin is locked by people who have forgotten their private key — That's equal to $140 billion. Losing access can be as simple as forgetting your password. Once you've lost your private key, it's unlikely you'll ever get it back. In 2021, hackers stole $600 million in crypto through PolyNetwork — the most significant single event crypto theft ever.

Accessing cryptocurrencies and NFTs indeed requires a private key. Still, these private keys can be hacked if used or stored on a networked device.

The Problem Of Link Rot

On top of it, NFTs are basically smart contract codes, and the vulnerability of code is known to anyone. A minor glitch and you may lose your valuable NFTs. NFTs include very little data by themselves, including functions like a deed to prove ownership, the artist's name, and the work's title. In essence, a collectible is usually linked with a URL.

What happens if the URL goes bad? Since maintaining the URL depends on the web host, the file is lost if the host goes out of business. The creator could also redirect the URL at any time. Many NFTs rely on InterPlanetary File System

(IPFS) to distribute files across multiple hosts and protect against a single host going under. Although NFT owners can choose to pay for ongoing hosting, no single party is responsible for maintaining the file.

Other challenges for NFT include:

Proper Education

The fundamentals behind NFTs might be too technical for non-technical users.

Volatility

There is a great deal of difficulty in estimating the price of the NFT due to its unpredictability. The value of a tokenized digital asset is set by the perceived value of the community rather than its functionality.

Every NFT's price will now be determined by its originality, scarcity of buyers and owners, and several other criteria. Prices for any type of NFT vary significantly because there is no defined standard.

People cannot predict the factors that may influence the price of NFTs. As a result, price swings remain constant, making NFT evaluation a difficult task.

Value

It is difficult to differentiate a valuable NFT from a valueless one as anyone can mint NFTs. Identifying valuable NFTs isn't sure; you'll have to do research to ensure what you're buying isn't worthless.

Liquidity

The NFT market suffers from liquidity issues. A seller must find a buyer willing to pay the perceived amount to make the sale. Since the price and worth of NFTs have no standard scale, it's difficult for buyers to decide on purchasing NFTs for just any price.

Gas Fee

For anyone to interact with the ETH Blockchain, they need to have enough 'gas'. As part of the transaction verification process, miners incur 'gas fees'. This is useful because it further develops security by keeping spammers from spamming the network. As gas fees vary, it's hard to get revenue after selling NFT with higher gas fees.

Environment

Minting and selling NFTs require computational works that are causing environmental problems.

Taxation

Trading NFTs is subjected to taxation, where the tax rate on selling NFTs can reach 28%.

Copyright Issue

Legal issues about intellectual property rights and copyright laws are also formidable setbacks for long-term NFT adoption. For example, you can encounter conflicts between pre-existing paper contracts and NFTs. Fraud can exploit newcomers by minting and selling copyrighted NFTs.

Legal Definition

In the entire world, there is no legal definition of NFT. Different countries, including the United Kingdom, Japan, and the European Union, are taking different ways to define NFT. The present laws on NFT are still trying to figure out what the correct definition is. As the market and variety of NFTs continue to expand, it is getting more challenging to establish a firm foundation for NFT compliance. This necessitates the creation of an international organization of non-fungible tokens to develop regulations and legalization throughout the world.

Selling Your NFT Without Delay

It's worth keeping in mind that minting your NFTs is actually just the beginning of the entire monetization of NFTs. With 19,5 million different tokens available on OpenSea, yours can easily get lost in the crowd quickly. Other well-known marketplaces don't differ from OpenSea either.

This is why, to find true success and offer NFTs to however many individuals as could be allowed, you should be shrewd about your advertising.

Assuming you're a deep-rooted craftsman with a reasonably measured following, this may not be that large issue. However, it could be difficult if you're just getting started and NFTs are your first foray into the online crafting market.

It is improbable that everybody will sell their new work of art for many dollars. Furthermore, hopping into this pattern aimlessly would be less than ideal.

Consequently, here are some ways to sell your NFTs quickly and immediately:

Utilize Your Imaginative Abilities

Whether it is a picture or a melody you are attempting to sell on the blockchain, your venture must come from imagination. With such countless individuals getting onto the fleeting trend, it takes a cautious wanting to stand apart from regular postings.

If you're uncertain where to start, try looking into the activities that others have proactively distributed. Interact with others who have sold their work of art for 1 or 2 Ethereum and inquire about how they did it. One striking thing about Web3 and NFTs is the local area perspective. Individuals are available to discuss their triumphs and their disappointments.

Furthermore, it is never damaging to inquire.

Join Communities

Joining a similar local area is the least demanding method for advancing your specialty and other computerized resources. These are Twitter, Discord, and Clubhouse. If you don't stay on top of the latest trends, you can be missing out on potential clients for your craft.

Communities like NFT Calendar feature forthcoming drops. This can be your beginning stage to see who is distributing the drop and what their local area joins are.

You can follow a couple of individuals in the space. In seven days, you will be aware of 100 others enthusiastic about this space.

Be Intentional

Assuming that you neglect to show certifiable interest in the Web3 development, it can feel like an outright drag to attempt to sell your NFT. Accordingly, it would most likely assist assuming you invest energy in finding out about crypto overall.

Are you genuinely enthralled with the prospect of a decentralized internet? Might you want to reside in a future where specialists can include their fans in their creative flow?

Although the development is still new, a ton occurs in the background. Also, showing an aim to learn and comprehend can rapidly draw similar individuals into your circle. These could likewise turn out to be individuals who will happily get one of your specialty pieces.

Promote Your NFTs on Social Media and Online Forums

Everyone is on social media, including your potential buyers. Thus, promoting your NFTs on social media and online platforms like Instagram, Telegram, Reddit, Twitter, and Facebook will help you sell your NFTs faster.

Instagram

Instagram is a stage for sharing computerized workmanship and photographs, making it the ideal platform for advancing your NFT assortment. A portion of the world's driving specialists use Instagram to gain publicity and get more eyeballs on their future deliveries.

Critically, advancing on Instagram is likewise more advantageous. You simply need to find pertinent hashtags and begin transferring photographs with them. Ensure you add numerous watchwords for each picture you transfer, and all the more critically, add pertinent subtitles.

To expand your span, it will be helpful if you explore useful related posts on Instagram.

There are additionally Instagram Reels, Highlights, and Stories that you can use to offer a sneak peek of sorts to your adherents. To gain more attention, try coming up with interesting Instagram Reels ideas.

Telegram channel

Telegram is a scrambled correspondence application that has been utilized by crypto-aficionados since its send-off. Obviously, it's an incredible platform for advertising your new NFT projects. However, there's an approach to this

Building trust and reputation is more important than merely posting the generic message "look at my NFT collection" on each channel you visit.

It's improbable that anybody will show interest given only these lines. All things being equal, attempt to assemble a story around your NFT collection. Draw in the gathering by educating them regarding an astonishing NFT collection you found, and afterwards present it to them.

It's a decent method for advancing your NFTs and creating more interest than ordinary methods.

Reddit

Another incredible stage where you can advance your NFTs is Reddit. Known as the "first page of the web," Reddit is a beautiful spot to promote your NFT assortment, essentially due to the number of individuals who use it.

Dynamic NFT financial backers frequently scour different subreddits to detect promising NFT projects early and get in at the base floor before the cost skyrockets. To become famous as an NFT maker, you basically can't disregard Reddit from your particular methodology.

Some well-known subreddits where you can purchase, sell, and advance NFTs include:

NFT

NFTsMarketplace

NFTExchange

NFTmarket

If you've been involved with Reddit for some time and have heaps of karma, your presents can produce more interest. While advancing on Reddit, you genuinely must make a legitimate picture.

Clients on Reddit are very sharp and will immediately recognize any inconsistent cases that you make in various subreddits. Ensure you have a good image of how you concocted the NFT assortment, what it addresses, and the guide it will probably take. That will assist you with making an accurate picture to individuals about what your NFT collection relies on.

Also, individuals love validness.

The most excellent NFT projects are ones with plainly characterized guides, far-reaching support, and a strong presence on various channels. These assists work with trust and produce esteem as financial backers comprehend how enthusiastic the makers are.

You want to do likewise. Utilizing a combination of these systems will undoubtedly get the job done. You could actually mint your NFT for nothing and sell it right away.

How To Source And Outsource Your NFT Art For Minting Or Listing

Sourcing for NFT arts is pretty simple but depends on how much you can search for NFT arts. You can get NFT arts minting from two different sources:

1. **Digital Artists**

You can become a digital artist by converting physical arts to NFTs. You will get such physical arts from various places and people by taking creative pictures and videos that appeal to people.

Within the NFT industry, artists utilize various art segments to create unique artworks. You can get your NFT Arts directly from digital creators by searching on Google, Twitter, Telegram channels and other online sites such as Rarity.tools or NFTcatcher.io for NFT art creators.

Prominent NFT artists in the industry include Beeple, Pak, XCOPY, Mad Dog Jones, and Cath Simard.

You can follow digital creators on various social media platforms and join their groups to source for their NFT arts.

2. Marketplaces

Your next option for sourcing NFT arts are NFT marketplaces, and there are a lot of them out there. Below is a list of where you can source NFT arts for listing:

AsyncArt

Axie Infinity

Crypto.com

Decentraland

KnownOrigin

MakersPlace

Mintable

Nifty Gateway

OpenSea

Rarible

SuperRare

The Sandbox

ThetaDrop

Valuables

Zora

CONCLUSION

NFTs have proven to be an exciting addition to the world of digital money. NFTs permit simple tokenization of physical and digital assets, opening up a vibrant new ecosystem where market participants can trade art, music, in-game items, etc. They use blockchain technology to handle the transaction and encode the identity of the owner of the NFT.

NFTs disrupt intermediaries, mitigate plagiarism and ensure authenticity and efficiency. They offer a lucrative technology with various benefits, including digital identity and marketing.

You can easily make 5-6 figures and change your life for the better by simply minting, buying and selling NFTs across NFT marketplaces. Creating wealth has never been easier than investing in NFTs. You can promote your brand and make quick money selling NFTs without delay.

However, various challenges confronting NFTs can be reduced or avoided by taking necessary measures. This book has covered all that you need to know about NFT and start making cool money easily.

www.ingramcontent.com/pod-product-compliance
Lightning Source LLC
Chambersburg PA
CBHW072106110526
44590CB00018B/3342